I Will No Longer Be Your Secret!

LOUICIANA JOSEPH

I Will No Longer Be Your Secret!

Copyright © 2023 Louiciana Joseph
All rights reserved.
ISBN: 798851054334

DEDICATION

This book is a tribute to those who have experienced the challenges of being in a hidden relationship. It aims to give you a voice and inspire healing and growth, allowing you to begin anew. I want to express my gratitude to my daughters for their unconditional love and unwavering support, which has helped me persevere through it all.

ACKNOWLEDGMENTS

I am grateful to acknowledge Michelle P Crump who encouraged me to pursue my dream of writing a book. Her words, "What are you waiting on? It's Time!" inspire me. My daughters, Dominque and Alexandria who also motivated me by saying, "Mom, you got this. We believe in you." Additionally, my family, friends and loved ones who has provided me with the necessary support and time to complete my work, which reveals a long-hidden truth.

Table of Content

Introduction 1

Chapter 1 – Meet and Greet But It's A Set Up……………………….3

Chapter 2 – Married Or Not? That's The Question………………....7

Chapter 3 – Trying To Get It By Manipulation & Control....................... 10

Chapter 4 – The Anointing Attracts 13

Chapter 5 – Crossing Boundries... 16

Chapter 6 – I Wasn't Running Ministry It Was Running Me 19

Chapter 7 - I'm Not The Only One………………………………...23

Chapter 8 - Bleeding But Yet Serving……………………………..26

Chapter 9 - I Is Married Narr! But Sshh! That's A Secret Too…………..30

Chapter 10 - Taking Accountability For My Actions…………………..33

Chapter 11- My Competition Became My Assignment…………………36

Conclusion.. 39

About the Author... 43

Introduction

The purpose of writing this book is to share my personal experience of being kept hidden in a relationship and the emotional distress it caused. I want to be transparent and truthful about my life, based solely on my experiences. My hope is that my story will encourage others to embrace their self-worth and refuse to be kept hidden in someone else's life. It's important to remember that you are wise, intelligent, beautiful, and present, and nobody has the right to make you feel otherwise. Hiding a partner or spouse in a relationship has become a common thing. Whether the connection is a platonic or erotic, it's essential to be valued and respected. If a private connection is consensual, it can grow and develop into a long-lasting healthy union. But if it's a secret, as in nobody should ever know, as it relates to non-existing, then here lies a big problem.

I value privacy and believe that individuals in relationships heading towards marriage should keep some things to themselves. It's important to avoid keeping secrets from each other as it damages the bond between partners. Personal matters should always be kept personal. It's okay to have secrets from outsiders, as long as there are no secrets between the two of you. I support a healthy, open relationship where partners are not afraid to display their affection in public and show their love to the world. You can still maintain privacy by choosing what, when, and how to share your passion with others. It's important to understand the difference between "private" and "secret" as these words have distinct meanings depending on the situation.

The term "private" refers to something that is not meant to be shared or made public. For instance, when two or more individuals have a private conversation, it should remain confidential between them and not disclosed to others. On the other hand, the term "secret" implies a deliberate concealment or non-disclosure of information, actions, or objects. While "private" is used to describe confidential matters, "secret" suggests a conscious effort to hide something. In a couple's relationship, having a secret or personal relationship might be acceptable if both parties agree to it for a reasonable amount of time. This allows the relationship to develop and mature without external interference. However, if there's no agreement, and the relationship is kept a secret for the wrong reasons, problems can arise. Individuals in secretive relationships maintain an outward appearance of being single while secretly maintaining an emotional or sexual connection with each other. It is unclear if either party is seeing anyone else because communication about the relationship is rare. Based on my experiences I've learned that secrets cause more harm than good.

When I found myself in a secret relationship, I questioned the love, longevity, authenticity, and strength of the connection. Inward conflicts arose from within that made me feel uneasy, fearful, and insecure. I doubt the authenticity of the relationship as well as my ability to be genuinely happy with the individual that demanded secrecy. The truth about being kept a secret is often due to deceit, embarrassment, and shame, all of which I experienced. When I said these words; "I will no longer be your secret!" my life began to change for the better.

Chapter One
Meet and Greet but It's a Setup

During a lunch with some female friends at a restaurant, one of them shared her experience of being prophesied to by a man of God who expressed an interest in establishing a church in South Florida. She spoke highly of his authenticity as a prophet and excellent character, which convinced us to meet him. We gathered with the man of God and his female cousin to hear about his ministry goals and the opportunity to join him in building his church. The meeting was intriguing, and he even prophesied to the group, delivering personal prophetic words before we left. I never experienced anything like it before. As we conversated with each other, one of the ladies suggested that she will speak to one of her Pastor friends on his behalf.

She would ask if the Man of God could use their building for service on the nights they were not having service, which she did, and the rest was history. During the lunch, one of the ladies told me that the man of God was single, and she thought he was interested in me. I politely declined and said that I was not looking for a relationship. However, it seemed that my response got back to him because he approached me and asked for my number. He expressed that he liked me, and we agreed to start a platonic friendship. Eventually, he asked me out on a double date with one of my friends who also attended his ministry and her fiancé. We went out to dinner and took a walk on the Hollywood Boardwalk. It was a pleasant and innocent outing.

During our conversation, the Man of God expressed interest in pursuing a more intimate relationship with me. He mentioned that he was single and searching for a wife. As a single woman hoping to find love and get married, I was intrigued. However, when he mentioned that he needed his papers, I became cautious. I understood that this meant he was in the United States illegally and needed a green card through marriage. I asked him to clarify his intentions and if he was only pursuing me for his papers. It's a valid question, isn't it? Were you interested in me or just wanted a green card? He reassured me that he truly liked me and hoped to build a future together. Despite my doubts, I chose to overlook the warning signs and attempt to sort through my emotions. I acknowledge that our relationship began on unstable grounds, with mixed signals and presumptions. However, I granted him the benefit of the doubt due to his kindness towards me. I believed he was authentic, sincere, and genuinely cared for me. I convinced myself that this man was perfect for me, not to mention he was a Man of God. His prophetic ministry was remarkably accurate, which meant he had no reason to deceive or lie to me or anyone else.

He's attempting to start anew in a foreign country and has been truthful about his situation; I respect that. I assumed he didn't have to reveal his status, but he did. This indicates that he doesn't keep secrets, particularly from someone he's pursuing. This is what we women who are broken do when we want something or someone bad enough. We see the right in the wrong, find the light in the darkness, and rationalize the most out-of-order circumstances. We speed up to pass the yellow lights and run through all the red to dysfunction and unhappiness when we crave Love, affection, and attention. We don't have to seek for this because it will find us. We attract who we are. Broken people attract broken people; it doesn't matter their status, title, or position in life, hence the saying, "Love is blind.

This person found me at a very venerable stage in my life. My last relationship did not end well, leaving me broken, with walls and barriers that only a skilled builder could knock down. In addition to that, I was not well in my body. I was always a sick person; even from childhood until now, I have suffered from type 1 diabetes. It's something that I've learned to live with for a very long time. Managing a disease can be tiresome and draining. It alters your mood and leaves you depleted for days and weeks at a time. I'm yet believing in God for my healing.

I have been plagued with depression for years, and having health issues makes me feel undesirable and unattractive. Those inner insecurities get the best of me at times, but I always knew I was beautiful on the inside and out. I never had a problem getting a man. I attract the wrong man at times. The attention that I received from this individual made me feel unique and special. I not only felt wanted, but he also made me felt needed. I have been in relationships before; this was not my first experience; however, it was different. This time it was a Man of God, with standard, and integrity, or so I thought. Through my experiences, I have come to understand that only a man who has God's heart can truly love purely and righteously.

Having God in your life does not guarantee that you will always do the right thing or behave properly, especially if you have not fully submitted yourself to Him. In the past, I have been hurt and broken by men, but this one was different because I had elevated him to the status of a servant of God and wrongly expected him to be a perfect leader. Unfortunately, he turned out to be a tyrant. When I realized that our friendship was heading in a direction I did not want, I shared my fears, hurts, and insecurities with him. This allowed me to gain clarity and understand what I did not want in a mate or a relationship. Being vulnerable can cloud our judgment and lead us to make poor choices that hold us captive in toxic situations for a prolonged period.

Chapter Two
Married or NOT? Now That's The Question!

It's true that not all men are the same. There are some who are genuinely good, with values, aspirations, and a strong sense of purpose. Unfortunately, there are also those who are only interested in short-term flings and have no intention of committing to anything meaningful. While I initially thought that my partner might be one of the former, it didn't take long for me to realize that he was a master manipulator. He wanted the benefits of a relationship without any of the responsibilities. Despite this, things started off well between us, and we even engaged in public displays of affection which boosted my self-esteem. However, I eventually came to see that his words and actions were nothing more than a facade.

I longed for something refreshing and unique, and this is what I envisioned. Words like "You look beautiful," "Your smile is lovely," and "I enjoy the way you make me feel" provided comfort to my soul and touched my emotions. It sparked both my intellectual and emotional senses, creating a sense of authenticity between us. With this newfound openness, I desired more and invested more into our bond by cleaning his house, washing his clothes, and ensuring his well-being. As our church grew, we held regular services and gained followers. News quickly spread that there was a Man of God in town, and people were drawn to the excitement of something new and different. Furthermore, members of the church were eager for prophetic words, always seeking validation for what they already knew in a prophetic way.

Just when I thought things were going smoothly and progressing in the right direction, everything came crashing down. During a church gathering, the Man of God mentioned his wife, surprising many of us who didn't know he was married. He then introduced her to the congregation, which left some of us confused and shocked. It turned out that he had already begun a relationship while being married, which was a huge red flag. Despite his explanation that it was a marriage of convenience, it was still a concerning situation for me and others. I couldn't help but wonder why he chose to disclose this information now and why I had to find out at the same time as the rest of the church. I felt hurt and betrayed that he had kept his marriage a secret for the two months we were dating. It was clear that he had been in a relationship with me while still committed to his wife. I was devastated as I had been investing my time and emotions in building a relationship with him. When I confronted him later in private about not telling me he was married, he responded that he was going through a divorce and that the marriage was not going to last. I couldn't believe what I was hearing. I emphasized that it didn't matter whether he was divorcing, he was still legally married, and that was disturbing and deceitful.

Within two months of knowing him, he failed to mention his wife and presented himself as a single man to his followers. He deceives not only me but also his congregation by casually introducing this woman without any indication of being married. This lack of accountability and disrespect to his followers is unacceptable for someone who claims to be a Man of God. Although this lady had her ministry, he attempted to merge the two churches, but it didn't work out. Every time we spoke, the topic of conversation was his deception, and we argued nearly every day. Despite his infraction, our relationship continued, and he persisted in convincing me that there was nothing sexual going on between them. I'm unsure if I can forgive him for his deceit.

I was enraged when I found out that they were living together. His communication with me while he was with her made me suspicious of his faithfulness. Despite my mixed emotions, I stayed in the relationship. They cohabited until the divorce was finalized. Proverbs 4:23 teaches us to protect our hearts, as it determines the course of our lives. Unfortunately, I failed to guard my heart and was caught off guard. This was my first time being romantically involved with a man of God, which presented a unique challenge for me. Though I knew what the Bible taught about relationships, it was difficult to judge the situation. I had to consider not only his character but mine as well.

Chapter Three
Trying To Get It Through Manipulation & Control

After the Man of God got a divorce, we went full speed ahead in our relationship. We were not dating during his short marriage, but the divorce gave us an excuse to take our feet off the brakes and move forward without reservations. I'm single; he's single, so why not? It was as if a burden was lifted. All red lights had officially turned green for me. The feelings between us grew more substantial, and our attitude changed. It didn't matter where we went together or what we did; we were single. Marriage was not a maybe, but now it had become a reality. I finally felt like we were now dating with a purpose. We became more intimate with each other. Now, let me say this to those of you that are reading this book, especially women, a proposal of marriage is not a license to have sex or behave in a manner that's unacceptable as a woman, and especially a woman of God.

A proposal of marriage or engagement is not marriage. Although we initially came together for ministry, our relationship evolved to focus on sex and intimacy. Despite this, I remained committed to church and the Man of God because I believed we were building something meaningful. As our bond grew stronger, I was given more responsibilities within the church he had founded. I proved to be reliable and kept things running smoothly, even when he was out of town doing ministry work. He made me feel like we were both investing in something great. I believed that once we got married, our secret affair would end, and we could move forward with a clean slate. However, I began to have doubts when I realized that he had proposed marriage without any engagement period.

This raised significant concerns for me, as engagement is an essential time for couples to get to know each other better and announce their intention to marry. It is also a promise between couples, symbolized by the engagement ring. However, in my case, there was no such commitment and when any conversation was bought to the front, it was passively avoided. Ladies, if a man promises you marriage, it is essential to remember that engagement should follow, even if it's a for a brief period. This allows both parties to prepare for their future together and alerts others of your commitment. Without preparation or obligation, it may be a red flag. In this relationship, I lost sight of myself and realized I was willing to give up everything for a false sense of security. The Bible often references cunning women, but men can also be cunning and crafty. From a young age, we are taught to aspire to become wives and many of us even plan our weddings before meeting a potential partner. Unfortunately, being single is not often seen as acceptable and can carry a sense of shame and disgrace for some women. This mindset may have contributed to why I held on for so long, as I did not want to be labeled as another single woman with a failed relationship.

There was such a longing for me to get married that it blinded me from the abuse I subjected myself to. Every abuser is not violently physical. Abuse is all about control and manipulation. If someone can control you, there's no reason for bodily harm. At times, I questioned who had the upper hand in our relationship. Control and manipulation can affect both parties in different ways. I believed that by doing everything my partner asked of me, he would eventually reciprocate and provide what I needed to maintain the relationship. However, I soon realized that I wasn't receiving the same consideration in return. The more I gave, the more he expected without putting in any effort to improve the relationship.

As women, we may attempt to manipulate situations to gain power, thinking we can make a man do what we want. But ultimately, it's important to recognize when we're not receiving the same level of love and respect in the relationship. I may have appeared submissive, but I viewed it as a means of gaining control. I believed my submission would lead me to the rewards I deserved for my hard work. I went to great lengths to prove my dedication to this man, but my efforts proved futile. It was not manipulation; I simply wanted to earn his love and respect. However, I have since learned that true love cannot be controlled or manipulated. Love exists on its own, and it cannot be forced. Men who manipulate are skilled at playing mind games, using clever and deceitful tactics to control and influence others for their personal gain. These tactics can range from covert to a more overt and aggressive approaches. Unfortunately, I have experienced all the above, including emotional blackmail, and gaslighting. These psychological tactics are used to gain power and control over another person. It is important to recognize and protect oneself from these manipulative, controlling behaviors. Manipulation is considered unethical and can have negative consequences for both the manipulator and the manipulated. It can damage relationships, erode trust, and result in feelings of anger, resentment, and betrayal. Throughout our relationship, I was increasingly resentful, but felt trapped.

Despite my attempts to break free, I kept getting pulled back in. You know you are in a tight grip if they can convince you to believe that they are all you need. Although he professed to love me, he would curse at me. Each time we got in an augment pieces of my heart died. Though I held him in high esteem, God kept showing me a different side of him. I was drawn to his anointing, gifts, and knowledge of the word of God, but I found his character unattractive. He was broken, and his moral compass was askew. I struggled to discern my wants and needs during our relationship. I now realize that my soul was entangled, and I did not know how to break free. As the word of God says, the gift and calling are without repentance, and all perfect gift comes from the Father above. The skills and anointing may be perfect, but we still need to be fixed. This man was on a different level than me. He was street-smart and spiritually inclined, which was both a blessing and a curse because he used it in a polluted manner.

Chapter Four
The Anointing Attracts

Have you heard the phrase "The Anointing Attracts" I have, and I've experienced it firsthand. The anointing not only draws people in, but it also captures their hearts. So, what exactly is the anointing? It's when someone is chosen and empowered for a specific purpose. This supernatural ability comes from the Holy Spirit and is often associated with healing, deliverance, and blessings through anointing with oil. It's also used for appointing officers based on the word of God in James 5:14-15. We may think many can be anointed without the Holy Spirit. The anointing is the Holy Spirit. 1 John 2:27 reads: "27 But the anointing which you have received from Him abides in you, and you do not need that anyone teach you; but as the same anointing teaches you concerning all things, and is true, and is not a lie, and just as it has taught you, you [a]will abide in Him."

It's important to understand that even someone who disobeys God and rejects the guidance of the Holy Spirit can claim to be anointed, but not by the Holy Spirit. The Devil can also mimic the working of the Holy Spirit, so it's crucial to have discernment within the body of Christ. Some people may operate under a different spirit that is not of God, but they may still refer to it as the Holy Spirit or the anointing of God. Satan has created a counterfeit kingdom that mirrors God's kingdom and its offerings. Many of us may be deceived because we allow the gifts bestowed upon man to cloud our judgment. When I first met the Man of God, he came in prophesying and displaying his gifts, which initially drew me in. However, as I continued to interact with him, I learned that the gifts are perfect because they come from God.

It's up to us to live clean and holy lives so that the gifts can flow through us without any hindrance or contamination. At first, I struggled to differentiate between the anointing and the man himself. I was so deeply moved by his presence that I had complete faith, hope, and trust in his ability to care for me - especially my heart. However, I eventually came to realize that the anointing draws attention to an individual and reflects positively on them. When we operate under the Holy Spirit's power, we undergo a physical and spiritual transformation. It's essential to never misuse God's glory for personal gain, especially capturing the hearts of vulnerable women. I once heard the man of God make a troubling statement about his ability to attract women due to his perceived anointing. He claimed that he could pursue any woman he wanted from anywhere in the world, and they would be attracted to him because of the anointing on his life. Unfortunately, this kind of attitude is not uncommon among religious leaders, particularly those of the prophetic because this gifts draws.

Anyone who believes that their anointing gives them the right to act without consequences is a renegade in the body of Christ. This type of behavior and mindset is unacceptable and can be very hurtful to others. When I heard this statement, I began to question what kind of anointing was drawing me to this person. Ultimately, I realized that true respect and integrity are the most important qualities to look for in a spiritual leader, not their gifts or appearance. I was drawn to a man who had a strong prayer life and called himself a prophetic warrior. He had a commanding presence and was able take charge of situations with ease. I admired his authority and looked to him for guidance and accountability, which gave me a sense of security. I felt like I had someone by my side who could handle anything. However, I failed to see the negative qualities that he possessed, such as lying, womanizing, and being a narcissist.

Despite his flaws, I was confident in his ability to pray for me and believed that his prayers would bring positive results. This caused me to become involved in a secret affair with him. I eventually realized that I had put too much faith in him, rather than in God, who is the ultimate source of all power and authority. It's true that opposites attract, but this can also lead to trouble when we seek something new and exciting. I was drawn to his culture, style, demeanor, and ability to have fun. We began dating, but I soon realized that it lacked purpose. Dating aimlessly is like driving without gas and expecting to reach your destination without breaking down. One day, I sat in quiet reflection and asked God, "Why me?" He replied, "Why not you, my daughter? Your heart is precious, so protect it and don't let just anyone in." I received a clear message to wait for a man who would treasure my heart. Despite my deepening feelings for my current partner, I realized it was only lust now that my eyes had been opened. Communication is key in building an authentic relationship. It's important to expose all parts of yourself to your partner, without anything hidden. A relationship is more than just going on dates and having sex. Hiding parts of yourself from your partner is unfair to both of you. Instead, connect on all levels; not just when things are going well, and not just when it comes to ministry.

Secret relationships can be disappointing and it's difficult to share your feelings with others when nobody knows about the relationship you are in. It's easy to feel weighed down by rejection. I once believed that kissing and holding hands in public was a sign of falling in love, leading to marriage. However, I eventually had to accept that those were just outward expressions that required no commitment or accountability. I questioned why God had allowed me to fall into a toxic relationship, but I realized that we attract people who are like us in some ways. I also had to ask myself what this person saw in me that drew an attraction. Was it a strong black intelligent woman? Or did he say to himself, there goes one right there; she looks vulnerable enough; she seems lonely, needy, and ready for love. Let's see if she will take the bait.

I learned through this experience that the enemy will always appeal to that side of us that is not entirely healed. He sees an opening; he's going for it. It does 't matter your status, position, nationality, gender, or race. He is not respectful of people. He comes to kill, steal, and destroy. At one point in our lives, we all have been broken, but we all are not hurt the same. Whatever brokenness that was not mended was used as an opening to my heart. This Man of God saw the door and took it.

Chapter Five
Crossing Boundaries

Crossing Boundaries is sleeping with a person you are not married to which is a relationship violation. You are not just connecting on a physical level but also on a spiritual one. Your soul gets intertwined. There is an entanglement that may not be impossible to break immediately, depending on the length of time you have been connected. That sexual encounter releases parts of you that enter that individual's mind, soul, and spirit. It's not just a laying down and getting up. It changes your life forever. This is why the word of God in Hebrews 13:4 (KJV) states that "Marriage is honorable in all, and the bed undefiled: but whoremongers and adulterers God will judge." When we as single women, fornicate, we sin against our own bodies.

Our bodies are the temple of the Holy Spirit. We should always protect our bodies, but most importantly, guard our hearts. Your heart is a gateway to your temple, and God honors marriage as a legal union that grants legal access to your spouse. When the Man of God and I first met, we felt an instant connection and closeness. Although we shared a bed, we did not rush into anything physical at first. When he said, "You are different," I confidently replied, "I don't rush into things easily. I don't know you well enough yet, so this is your side of the bed, and this is mine." This was our first trip away from home, and we were alone in a hotel room hundreds of miles away. Despite being alone together, we respected each other's space and boundaries that night.

I believe one of the reasons I agreed to take our relationship to the next level, as it pertains to being sexually engaged, was because of my lack of commitment to God. Looking back, I had a bad case of having a form of godliness which allowed me to make excuses for my actions. I really did not take my spiritual life seriously. Because of this posture, I was quickly captivated and held hostage to a false sense of security. I came across a passage of scripture in the word of God that spoke to my situation at the time. 2 Timothy 3:5-7 "Having a form of godliness but denying the power thereof: from such turn away. For of this sort are they which creep into houses, and lead silly captive women laden with sins, led away with divers lusts, Ever learning, and never able to come to the knowledge of the truth." (KJV) This was me; I was that silly woman that was taken captive by my own lust and entice but to be more clear, I decided to read the Amplified Bible, which breaks it down for me. "Holding to a form of [outward] godliness (religion), although they have denied its power [for their conduct nullifies their claim of faith]. Avoid such people and keep far away from them. For among them are those who worm their way into homes and captivate morally weak and spiritually-dwarfed women weighed down by [the burden of their] sins, easily swayed by various impulses, always learning, and listening to anybody who will teach them, but never able to come to the knowledge of the truth."

The word of God found me, and I was desperately in need of deliverance. I allowed the Man of God to enter my heart during a time when I was morally, spiritually weak, and immature. I was already struggling with my own personal issues which made it easy to give in to his advances. At one point, I thought I might be pregnant, but I had mixed feelings about it because of the uncertainty of bringing a child into the world. The Man of God was unhappy when he heard the news and immediately suggested that I should start thinking about what to do if I was pregnant. He even stated that he regrets we got involved now that there's a possibility of a baby. I was shocked by his cold and abrupt response, as I never thought he would suggest having an abortion.

The fact that I didn't usually have a cycle made me think getting pregnant was next to impossible. I decided to go to the doctor to calm my nerves. The doctor told me I wasn't pregnant which ended my nightmare. A week and a half later, my cycle came on. I was relieved and disappointed at the same time. The disappointment for me came because it would have torn us apart, instead of bringing us together. In some ways, I believe I was in the relationship alone. This was another red flag waving in my face but off course I ignored it. To tell me to get an abortion, which is against our faith, should tell me how far he would go to protect his image. It pains me to admit this, but I was still being spiritually developed in Christ when I met the Man of God. I was a grown, matured woman in many things but when it came to spiritual matters, I was very much immature and ignorant of spiritual things. I've come a long way and still coming into the fullness of God.

Being around the Man of God opened my spiritual appetite and made me crave more of God. I witnessed the gifts in action, including healing, deliverance, and prophetic declarations. Seeing these manifestations made me hunger for God's presence like never before. I knew that the gifts and calling are without repentance, but I was being converted. There were times I talked to God and him to help me. I was aware that I had personal issues that needed to be addressed, but I couldn't seem to resolve them. My actions did not align with the person I wanted to be, and I found no pleasure in what I was doing any longer.

I felt a sense of guilt and started blaming myself for everything that was going wrong in my life. Eventually, I confided in the Man of God, expressing my concerns about our actions being morally wrong. However, it felt like I was talking to a wall, as nothing seemed to change. I acknowledge that I too was at fault for not respecting boundaries. We didn't respect any boundaries we tried to set for each other. During times of loneliness, I longed for intimacy and was always given a yes. However, we were both using each other for convenience to satisfy our flesh. In the world I avoided these type of men, but I was confronted with the same type of man in the church, which was unexpected. This was my first time being with a Man of God, but I only reaped hurt, pain, and anger.

Chapter Six
I Wasn't Running Ministry; It was Running Me

Have you ever participated in a race where the objective is to reach the finish line without collapsing? I was in a similar situation where I felt the pressure and force of a race without making any real progress. The reason behind this was because I had been keeping a secret that was eating away at my soul, causing emotional instability. I found myself crying, worrying, and feeling depressed. I even lost weight because of it. This thing affected every aspect of my life, including my ability to serve in ministry. Despite not enjoying it, I continued to serve. Whenever I heard negative things about the Man of God, it affected my progress.

I wanted to retaliate and hurt him, but he acted as if everything was okay. The only hope I had was that there was someone out there who would love me unconditionally. I worked as a pastor for four years while under his leadership. During that time, I took on various roles including armor-bearer, housekeeper, personal assistant, psalmist, and financial advisor. I was happy to help wherever I was needed. We often traveled together, and sometimes people mistook me for his wife, but I would decline to sit next to him so as not to give the wrong impression. There were occasions in which I had to be his personal chauffeur, but when I fell ill, he still anticipated my presence despite my indisposition. This left me feeling taken for granted.

I felt like ministry was doing a job on me and not the other way around. Regrettably, it was all about him and less of me. I soon discovered that the ministry did not prioritize the development and guidance of individuals towards their calling. It was primarily fixated on prophetic movements with little emphasis placed on spiritual growth. The Man of God was more focused on preaching, prophesying, and collecting offerings than on mentoring his members or myself. While it's important to seek salvation, if you find yourself in a ministry that prioritizes your finances over your spiritual growth, it's best to leave and never look back. My role in the ministry was clearly defined, but I wasn't sure if it was beneficial for me. I started off singing and then ended up counting money, eventually being given the responsibility of opening, and closing the church and leading prayers, even when there was no service. When the church moved, I was entrusted with the keys to the new building. When the Man of God was away for extended periods, it was up to me to keep the ministry going. The challenge of taking on the responsibility of preaching in the Man of God absence weighed heavily on my shoulders.

I also had to ensure that guest speakers were properly compensated when funds were insufficient. Despite the members' limited participation when he was not present, I felt a sense of belonging and purpose in shepherding them. However, leading a group of people whom I did not give birth to was not without its difficulties. I knew that the people needed a shepherd, but I struggled to fill the Man of God shoes. Moreover, the dynamics of our relationship changed when we became secret lovers. Despite these challenges, I persevered and continued to embrace my responsibilities. After building trust with me, the Man of God would often disappear for extended periods of time, reappearing only occasionally. Everything was not all negative because when my car broke down, the Man of God provided me with a vehicle to use.

While I appreciated the gesture, I was left wondering if there was a hidden motive behind it, given that he owned multiple cars. There was a shift in our relationship when he began to distance himself from me in public. Our ability to ride in the same vehicle was now limited and our time together was restricted except when being his driver to his assignments. On one occasion I was expected to drive back home after a long day of his preaching out of town. As we head back to the city, the Man of God was chatting and laughing on his phone, while everyone else was making small talk and drifting off to sleep, relieved that they didn't have to drive. I couldn't take it anymore so; I pulled the car over. I expressed my frustration not caring who was in our company. I was the only one doing everything in ministry and I was tired!! I yelled to the top of my lungs, "And I'm not driving another mile in this car! I thought you were tired Man of God? I thought you said you were going to take a nap. But you are on face-book, texting, and making calls to everyone you know. We won't get home tonight! and I don't have a problem calling my job and telling them I can't come in to work in the morning!" The weight was too much for me to handle. At this point, I didn't consider this serving in ministry, but rather, someone taking advantage of my love and support. This was clearly the result of him feeling entitled and thinking that the world revolved around him.

I was viewed by him and the people he shepherds as being responsible for everything. No one else shared the burden, and it was becoming unbearable. I finally realized this wasn't God's work, but the work of man, and it required a lot of time, effort, and money. The Man of God believed I was going crazy, but I was experiencing a mental breakdown. I stepped out of the car, left the keys in the ignition, opened the back door, and politely sat down. I gave those that accompanied us the option to take over. The Man of God got out the car, approached the driver's seat and began driving without asking anyone to help. Then he began his ranting. "What's wrong with you? Are you crazy?" I yelled back, No! But you're a** is crazy! I'm tired of all yawl! And I'm tired of you!! I have a job to go to in the morning, something that no one in that vehicle considered!"

We drove all the way back trying to avoid what happened. It's interesting that he would prefer to drive himself rather than ask anyone else besides me to help. I assumed he needed time to break down their self-esteem and self-worth in order to do that. This was the first time I was heard. I believe that night I regained my voice and myself self-respect because I put actions behind my words, and it felt good. Ministry can be challenging at times and to feel unqualified makes it even harder. Despite my lack of qualifications and experience, I was appointed as an assistant pastor to keep the congregation together during his absence. I realize that if I was to do this job effectively, I would need to educate myself in this area of expertise; therefore, I enrolled in bible school to feel more deserving of the position. Even though I was going through tough times, the acts of kindness I received made me feel appreciated. Looking back, I realized that these actions were all part of a bigger plan. Sometimes, it felt like I was not doing ministry, but rather, the ministry was using me. Although I had the option to leave, I hesitated because of the involvement of other people. In addition, I loved ministry and being a part of something good. My vulnerability was capitalized on, but I needed to be needed. In some way I felt and believed all the mistakes, misfortunes, trials, struggles and disappointments was grooming and preparing me for something greater.

Chapter Seven
I'm Not The Only One!

After two and a half years of keeping a secret, I realized that things weren't going to improve. It felt like a never-ending cycle, like running on a treadmill without making progress. I had numerous conversations and arguments about how I was being treated and what I was sacrificing without receiving anything in return. My social circle was small, but I confided in a close friend who listened without judgement. Her support kept me grounded and sane during a difficult time. Without her, I'm not sure how I would have coped. Some days, I felt lost and unsure of what to do next. I began to question every decision and action I made. Additionally, I heard rumors about the Man of God's infidelity, which caused me to go into depression.

If there were discussions of his inappropriate behavior, then that proves it wasn't a secret between us after all. However, it is common for people to have secrets that they believe only they know about. This is the lie we tell ourselves to justify our actions. Although the rumors were true, I remained composed upon hearing the news because the Man of God was my Pastor, not just my secret lover. Since I thought no one knew, I did not engage with the rumors and hoped I would not be associated with those women. Whenever someone mentioned the gossip, I either walked away or disregarded it based on who was speaking or how it was conveyed.

Those who spread the news talked to me directly, but I questioned if they shared it because they knew we were close or involved in a secret affair. Nevertheless, I did not allow it to affect me. At first, I felt disgusted and irritated when he confided in me about his multiple affairs, but I kept my feelings to myself. Unfortunately, my suspicions were confirmed when I found out that someone else I knew was also involved with him. I learned about it through hearsay, which is often how bad news spreads. This situation put a strain on our relationship, and I found myself drifting away from my faith due to the emotional turmoil. To make things worse, he began to speak to me disrespectfully, demanding rather than asking me to do things. His behavior was like that of a spouse, which made me very uncomfortable. At this point, I realized that I had sunk to his level by responding with swearing and shouting instead of taking the high road, as Michelle Obama suggested; "When they go low, we go high." Despite his status as a Man of God, I lost all respect for him because of his behavior. He was a narcissist who believed that God would not hold him accountable for his wrongdoings and that he could do as he pleased without consequences.

He saw himself as a superior being and me as someone beneath him. He didn't think his actions would have consequences with God or society. He acted as if I was the one who needed redemption, however, I received a call from a woman claiming to be in a relationship with him. I was surprised and asked why she was contacting me, why she hadn't told me earlier if she knew about us, and what had changed. She admitted that she wanted to share this information with me but didn't know how. She found a hotel key card with my name in his pocket when he visited her once. While I couldn't recall us paying for a hotel room, I couldn't rule it out, since we had shared rooms before. What hurt more was that this woman was a friend from church, and we had never talked about him or confirmed our relationship; however, she had already told several pastors about their affair.

As usually I confronted him, but he denied it. This was on a day we were planning to take a trip together. We wanted to spend some quality time away from all the noise. While preparing and packing at his house, I decided to boil some water to make tea. I threw the hot boiling water at him when he came through the door. I missed him, of course, and was glad I did. I might have been in jail today if that water had hit his face. His response made me felt so dirty about the ordeal: "Man, that was just a thing of convenience." I responded, "So you went with her sexually because you needed a place to stay?" He said it was a one-time thing, but she adamantly stated that it was more than that. At this point, it didn't matter whether it was once, two, or three times. I thought I was in a committed relationship with the Man of God, but his reasoning puzzled me. He convinced me that it was normal to have feelings for someone else, and made it sound like it was a common occurrence. However, I later found out that the woman who approached me had done so because she had developed feelings for him. This made being in the same church unbearable for both of us. On one occasion, I had asked the woman to assist with the service, but she refused, stating that she was not right with God and did not want to play with Him. I realized that this was a passive-aggressive attack on me because I was overseeing everything.

Despite her indirect insult, I was always able to sense what she was trying to convey. It was unfortunate that both of us was dating the same man, in the same ministry, and at the same time. It seemed like I was the only one that felt like something was wrong with that picture. I came to the realization that this secret was being discovered slowly but surely because this Man of God couldn't remain committed to no one, not even God.

Chapter Eight
Bleeding But Yet Serving

Although we were yet connected things eventually began to slow down off course. You cannot have all these indiscretions and keep up the momentum of a relationship. I was burned out! I started coming to church late on purpose because I didn't like how the Man of God treated me. His tone got dominating and aggressive. I will never forget that day we were having a conversation about our relationship and ministry, he shouted at me and told me to shut up. I almost strike at the Man of God but something in me held me back. His philosophy was that he talked, and I listen, no response, just listen. "When I talk, you need to be quiet, and you need to listen to me." This was the straw that broke the camel's back for me.

I was driving him from an event, and in that moment, I felt like crashing the car. I stated to him that the only reason I won't crash his car, is because I was in it too and I did not want to hurt myself. I felt like I was no longer working for the Lord, but for him. There were times I came to church early and got upset because I really did not want to be there. All my joy was gone. One time I picked up a member for church and was on time. I dropped them off and told them I forgot something at home. I drove to the back of the building and parked my car. I sat there eating boil peanuts until service had started. I did not go in until it had reached midway. I started to have regrets, praying for the pain to go away but it was a slow and painful process.

Although we had physically stop having sex; my mind, soul, and spirit was still tied to the Man of God. One day after rehearsing for weeks in my mind what I would say to the Man of God, I decided to call. I believed that there was a silent cognizance between us that indicated that things had ended, but it was never official. There was so many lose ends. When I called the Man of God the fire within me burned. "I don't know what you got to do or what you got going on, but you need to meet me, and meet me now! What I have to say is very important and if you don't meet with me now, you'll see me in church, and I don't think you want that to happen." I was so angry at this point, especially after talking to the young lady. I was willing to put the truth out there and let the chips fall where they may. I was ready to tell the church, social media, family, and friends that me and the Man of God were screwing each other. I felt that he had more than me to lose anyway. I guess that scared him. He then replied, "You don't have to do all that; you being extra!" My response was: "Let me tell you something, N**ger! If you don't meet me today, I'm telling you, you'll see a side of me you have never seen before!

You will be held accountable for your actions, and everyone will know what you have done, including what we did together. The way you treated me is unacceptable, and I will not allow you to treat another woman the same way. Face the consequences of your actions and meet with me. We met at a restaurant, and despite his attempts to act unaffected, he couldn't hide the fact that he was a narcissist. He arrived on his phone, glanced at me, and simply said, "You look good." He hugged me from the side and patted my shoulder as if I were a child. I could tell he was unsure whether to stay away from me or embrace me, so his actions had no effect on me. I informed him that I did not want a hug because I was there for business. We went inside to order food, but I was too angry to eat.

However, he made matters worse by constantly checking his phone, which infuriated me even more. I demanded that he put his phone away and give me his undivided attention if he wanted to have a serious conversation with me. We argued back and forth, and I expressed my frustration with his tendency to bring up past conflicts whenever he gets upset. "I need to be honest with you. Your actions are unacceptable and cannot continue. People need to be aware of how you live and conduct yourself in ministry. Your behavior is reckless and lacking in any signs of repentance. When you ask me to preach or participate in ministry activities, I felt compelled to fast in order to prepare myself. I would never lay my hands on anyone if we had sex the night before. I have told you this multiple times, yet you continue to act as though you are without sin. Your actions have made it difficult for me to perform, minister, or sing because I feel so guilty about my own sins. I am exhausted and cannot continue to hold a grudge against you. However, if this behavior continues, I will be forced to distance myself from you. Your actions have caused me unimaginable pain, tearing my heart into pieces that cannot be easily mended. I trusted you with my heart when I exited my last relationship, and you have broken that trust in the most hurtful way possible. I bared my soul out to you. You knew what I had to endure in my previous relationships. I was looking to you for guidance and protection as a Man of God, but you turn around and do to me the same things the unsaved men did and even worse.

You're just as bad as the rest of the Ni ***gers out there on the streets. You aren't any better than them. During a conversation, you mentioned that if a person did something wrong, they could seek forgiveness from God, and he would listen. However, you have repeatedly used this to elevate yourself and belittle me, claiming that God hears your prayers but not mine because in your eyes you the King and I'm the damsel in distress. This behavior is unbecoming of someone who claims to be a prophet of God and has left me feeling emotionally wounded. I hope you understand how your words and actions impact others. The relationship left me spiritual traumatized that I trusted no one in ministry. I was angry, bitter, spiritually broken, battered, and bruised. I was so afraid to go to any ministry because I felt like someone would judge me. I felt very condemned.

After our meeting, I took out his key and said to him' "I'm sorry, I won't be needing this anymore." He said, "What do you mean?" I replied, "Just what I said, did I bite my tongue? I won't be needing these anymore." And I gave him his keys. I believe that the Man of God did not take me seriously when I gave him back his keys because he thought I was coming back to church after that meeting; however, this was the beginning of the end for both of us. People from church were calling my phone because they saw I was absent which was unusual, but I was so hurt, so I advise a few of them that repeatedly called, to stop calling because I was not coming back, and I was done the ministry.

Chapter Nine
"I Is Married Narr!" But Sshhh! That's a Secret Too

In the early stages of our relationship, the question arose about his true intentions - was he interested in me, for who I was, or was it solely to obtain his citizenship? Of course, he responded that he was interested in me, and who I was; however, as the relationship progressed, I agreed to marry him for immigration purposes. Several months later, we attended the immigration interview for which I pretended to be a happy and in-loved wife. We took several pictures as evidence to make it seem real. However, it was all a façade. Our wedding wasn't the typical kind with rings, flowers, or cake. Instead, it was more like a business transaction for which I received no compensation for my participation.

I believe that the Man of God acted out of his own selfish desires and had an alternative motives from the beginning. The love he offered was false and the relationship was toxic. I was too deeply involved to see it. After facing the undeniable truth, I realized that I had wasted time, years, and investments on something that wasn't real. I felt like I wouldn't have gotten into this relationship if I had known better. I believed I was doing well until I became involved with him. He contaminated the purity of my calling, which I had worked hard to maintain. I knew if I was ever going to get out of this with some shred of dignity, I had to learn how to forgive myself.

Unfortunately, our marriage did not last but it was not intended to nor did my sacrifice acknowledged but we hung in there for a year, after which, I couldn't take it anymore, so I asked him to file for a divorce. A ring with no commitment is a lie, and I couldn't continue lying to myself anymore. Our relationship was doomed from the start - just a mere fluke and a false sense of security. I was in denial for a very longtime, pretending that our connection was genuine, but deep down I knew that it wasn't. The only one that benefited was him, and not me. I was addicted to the dysfunction of our so-called love, but eventually, I realized that I needed to get off the merry-go-round. He always entertained other women, made me hold down a church, and now, convinced me to marry him, solely to stay in this country, it was becoming too much. It was exhausting for me to render any type of quality support to him and the few members he pastored, especially since we had to keep our relationship a secret. Despite his efforts to keep it under wraps, news spread that we were married. In the beginning of our relationship, we enjoyed each other's company and had meaningful conversations about marriage. However, as I stated in my previous chapter, as time went on, it became clear that he had lost interest in me and started pursuing other women.

Even though I longed for love and companionship, I realized that I couldn't force someone to reciprocate my feelings. Everyone did not know we were married but there was enough gossip to make people curious. One day, while grocery shopping with my daughters, a woman approached me and loudly asked if I was still married to the man of God. I felt so embarrassed and so did my daughters. I didn't know how to respond, and it seemed like she wanted to make sure everyone heard her. From then on, things were different, and I slowly started to drift away. This situation ended up costing me more than I was willing to lose. Sometimes, the Man of God would call to chat or check-in, but I didn't always feel like talking. I didn't want to hear anything, no excuses, or pretending as if he really cared about me. There were times I just went mute because I didn't have the strength to fight anymore. People tend to check-in with you to see if you're still standing, so him calling me didn't change my perception of him.

Chapter Ten
Taking Accountability For My Actions

I remembered feeling so lost and helpless, constantly repeating to myself, "God, I don't know what to do. You got to get me out of this." It was a difficult time for me, and I knew I had to learn to forgive myself before I could move on. I felt like I had lost myself and didn't recognize who I was anymore. I told myself that this isn't the person I was meant to be. I had been struggling for so long, so I prayed to God for guidance. I realized that I also played a role in the situation and didn't want to blame the Man of God entirely. By taking responsibility for my actions, I opened the door for God to assist me in forgiving him. Although he may have taken advantage of the situation, I was also longing for love and acceptance.

I couldn't put all the blame and shame on him, knowing that our actions were not right. I wanted to change and be different but didn't know how to do it. Sometimes in life, you must be tired of being sick and tired. I got to the point where I was so tired I felt like I was stuck, not moving, or progressing any longer. I felt like I had a hole in my heart and couldn't take it anymore. I felt helpless not knowing how to let go, and powerless to my own desires. I knew It was not healthy, so I prayed and talked to God every chance I got. I can say by the grace of God, I got out of it. I had a very close friend that encouraged me to leave. I was venting to her just about every chance I got. At one point I became spiteful, vengeful, and bitter. I thought to myself, what can I do to hurt him? I was so distraught, I thought of all types of evil ways to get him back for trapping me.

I became so focus on that; I thought I was losing my mind. I thought about taking my case to social media, the court of public opinion. I was willing to put the business out there and let everybody know that I and him were together, physically, emotionally, and sexually. I had to rethink that because when I really thought about it, I would not only destroy his character, but mine as well. What I went through, I wouldn't wish on my haters. I knew I had to make a change. I didn't want my daughters going through what I've been through. I needed to show them that I was a God-fearing woman who could overcome and admit her mistakes. Being a secret hurts. It gives the other person power and control over your life, allowing them to do whatever they want, whenever they want, and for as long as they want. How can you get help when you're sworn to secrecy. My prayer was always a cry for help, but you can't be healed from what you choose to hide. I made-up my mind that I was no longer going to hurt. And that's how I end up coming out of it. I literally had to make a choice. No one pulled me out, despite my cry. I made the decision to not live a life of secrecy any longer.

Enough was enough! When I felt like I had enough and could not bear another day of pain, my process of deliverance began. What was interesting about that was that I was struggling and felt like I was drowning in the dysfunction, while the other person was catching flights, travelling, doing business and ministry as usual as if it was just another day at the office and church. To say I was in unchartered waters was an understatement. Trying to survive in a sea of infested water, while they had moved on to the next curvy shaped, intelligent, independent, vulnerable victim. My eyes opened to the fact that this individual was used to this type of lifestyle. Fathers sleeping with their daughters is not a new phenomenon. Eli's sons, Hophni and Phineas died because of it. They were the priest that slept with the women of the temple.

God told Eli to correct his sons, but he didn't, and it cost them their lives. This is something that has been going on for ages. However, we as women has a responsibility to stay in God, and keep ourselves holy, no matter how anointed a Man of God is. I had to take accountability for my actions. I'm the one that was having a nervous breakdown because I gave my soul to someone that was not my husband. I'm the one that was not eating, sleeping, and losing weight. Therefore, I had to get my house in order, and as time progress that's exactly what I did. From my perspective, I was dealing with a narcissist.

One day, we had a disagreement on our way to church. Despite my anger, he acted as if nothing had happened and carried on with the service. He asked everyone to pray while I refused to participate. I would have left if I had my own transportation. He told everyone that if we are not walking and praying, we are being disobedient and had a demon. He tried to lay his hands on me because I refused to obey his instructions. I did not want his hands on me in no way, shape, or fashion, those days was over. I was still upset about one of our earlier blowouts. He told the deacon to hold me down because I had a demon that needed to be cast out. Well, that night, that deacon found out who was more stronger. It was a mess! His behavior and response to the entire situation hurt and embarrassed me.

How can anyone attempt to cast a demon out of the person they are having a sexual affair with? Only a person with a narcissist attitude would do something like that and then try to justify their actions. He never apologized for that incident or felt any remorse. This was easily swept under the rug, so the disrespect worsened. You know, a narcissist is someone that believes that what they are doing is always right. They justify every wrong move or mistake in their lives. They never take accountability for their actions. They convince themselves that they are right and that others involve is wrong, even though they're the ones that's victimizing everyone else. They want you to apologize to them, and they feel justified when you do. It's hard to heal in the place you're being abused.

And it's hard to heal and move on if you are tied to a narcissist. Serving in the ministry while catering to others made it almost impossible to heal. I was in charge, but I was spiritually hemorrhaging. Leading and bleeding though the hurt, even when I didn't feel like it. I kept on doing it, until I made that final decision not to.

Chapter Eleven
My Competition Became My Assignment

Sometimes we pretend that a well-known fact is a secret just to shield ourselves from the painful truth. But it's important to face reality, even if it's uncomfortable. In my case, finding out that I was not the only one sleeping with the same man was painful, however, I soon realized that my competition became my assignment. I now had to help this woman break away from the relationship that she thought was a blessing. It's important to note that I had no romantic intentions towards the Man of God at this point. We had both realized that our connection with him was unhealthy. This woman was in tears before me, expressing disbelief at how this man had treated us unfairly. I felt embarrassed and ashamed but tried to comfort her.

We were both in ministry and used to be friends, but her secret of being in a relationship caused distance between us. I advised her that she should have approached me earlier if she suspected my involvement. Although I felt betrayed, I realized that she was not the issue - the Man of God who mistreated us was. She asked how I moved on so quickly, but I informed her that it was not an overnight process. I prayed daily to God for help in recovering my self-respect and dignity. I told her that deliverance takes time, and one must be willing to walk away from what God has delivered them from. She desired more than just a one-night stand, but he did not reciprocate her feelings. The more I talked with her the more she cried and poured out her heart. She was being transparent and very apologetic. I was moved with compassion and empathy towards her.

Then I started to get very angry and outraged for the both of us. We were victims, crying and worrying over the same man. In that moment, I made up my mind that it was completely over. By ministering to this young lady, it forced me to look at my own situation. It gave me the spiritual strength and fortitude to stand in the grace God had extended to me. I felt empowered as I spoke life into her. I saw a lot of myself in her so as I'm telling her, she's better than that, or she deserve someone to love her unconditionally, I was speaking to myself. The conversation ended that day on a good note and so did our friendship. I understand that forgiving others can be difficult, especially when they have hurt you. It can also be tough to forgive yourself when you feel like you've done something wrong. Jesus once said that if we don't forgive others for their mistakes, then our heavenly father will not forgive us. However, once you learn to forgive yourself, it becomes easier to forgive others. It's important to note that forgiving someone doesn't necessarily mean you have to let them back into your life. Forgiveness is ultimately for your own well-being and personal growth, and it can help release any negative emotions you may be holding on to.

I carried so much anger that manifested in how I responded to him and life itself, but as soon as I forgave, that anger left. My response seemed lighter to conditions. It's imperative to let go and have closure of a toxic relationships. You may never get to talk to the person again or make that last phone call to make a clean break. Things may end on a bitter, sour note, but you can write a letter to yourself. Say everything you need to say to that person, and then burn it, set it on fire. Let that represent you destroying everything that came to kill you. Release it and let it go. Sometimes people will hold you hostage to your pain, hurt, and anxiety, not allowing you to speak about your feelings.

However, you can take back your life and get back in control. Forgiving and releasing someone can be done in countless ways, but ultimately it's up to you to choose what feels right to you. If you're uncertain, I suggest praying and seeking guidance from God. However, it's important to remember that I am not the ultimate authority on this matter. It's crucial to never confront the person in private or alone, and to always have a support system in place. I had the courage to confront the Man of God who had wronged me, and while I didn't expect an apology, I did apologize for any wrongdoing on my part. There are people who take advantage of person's vulnerabilities by exploiting their weaknesses to get what they want. In this case, the Man of God in question knew how to manipulate this woman by making her believe as a prophet his every words was to be respected, whether wrong or right. She was literally afraid that something would happen to her if she went against his wishes. It's crucial to understand that allowing someone to disrespect you may encourage them to continue doing so. As someone who doesn't tolerate such behavior, I make sure to shut it down immediately. However, leaving a toxic situation can be difficult. Leaving a toxic environment doesn't necessarily mean the path moving forward will be obstacle-free. At times, I would let the phone ring and allow my voicemail to take the call. The issue with the other woman was that she consistently answered the phone, sometimes on the first ring.

I made it clear to her that this was not acceptable. Despite feeling intimidated by him, she believed that something terrible would happen to her if she did not comply. We had numerous counseling sessions to instill courage, and strength in her so she can hand the confidence to move on. In the process, I believe that God was strengthening my faith and giving me the courage to mentor her through her struggles. I thank God for the opportunity to be used to help this woman who was going through the same struggles I endured. Healing was administered through transparency and honesty. While ministering to her strengthened my personal relationship with God and confirmed that I made the right decision to move on as well. She came in my presence feeling broken, but left feeling empowered, forgiven, and free to forgive.

It's amazing how Jesus can forgive us for everything, yet we struggle to forgive those who wronged us. God is the ultimate healer, way maker, and miracle worker. Sometimes, we experience things that we never thought we would get over. We may question when, why, and how did we get ourselves into so much trouble. We may feel stuck with no way out at times. However, we must remember that God is faithful through it all and he is always in control. We must take responsibility for our actions, and always be willing to forgive others. After all, God forgave us.

Conclusion

In this book, I reveal my personal and private experiences in the hopes of helping others. To help others, we must first be honest with ourselves and those around us. Honesty leads to healing, and healing brings new life. Unfortunately, many women lack the necessary tools to navigate through dangerous relationships, especially when dealing with a manipulative partner who exhibits narcissistic tendencies. My mission is to help as many individuals as possible escape toxic and abusive relationships by exposing the secrets of these destructive partnerships. When I say, "I will no longer be your secret," I'm referring to the mistaken belief that one's actions and behavior go unnoticed or unimportant to others.

I want to help people understand that their actions and choices impact those around them. I used to deny rumors and suspicions, thinking that it will fade away, but it didn't. Many people are afraid to talk about their experiences, but I decided to share mine so that I could live a life that aligns with my faith. In Luke 22:32, Jesus told Peter that he would pray for him so that he wouldn't lose faith, and that he should strengthen others once he had returned. This means that we should share our stories of redemption and help others who are struggling. Sharing my truth allowed me to break free from the stigma, and it can do the same for you. We can never change what we do not acknowledge. Yes! I did it, Yes! I slept with the Man of God, and he slept with me, and we slept with each other.

This is called total confession, acknowledgment, and repentance. This is how renewal starts and deliverance begins. No more hiding and sweeping our sins under the rug. One confession at a time will make big changes. The word of God tells us, if we confess our sins, he is faithful and just to forgive us of our sins and cleanse us from all unrighteousness. (1John 1:9) Yes! I did it! I sinned! I take full responsibility for every bad decision that got me in the trap I was in. Am I in that trap or situation today? No! Did God forgive me? Have I forgiven myself? Absolutely! I am not the first nor the last to experience a setback like this. However, I am certain that God's grace is all-encompassing. His strength is most evident in our moments of weakness. If we do not share our stories of triumph, we will remain trapped in the enemy's web of shame, blame, doubt, and deceit. We will continue to be haunted by negative self-talks that make us feel inadequate, unworthy, and abandoned. The opinions and judgments of others do not matter as much as our own. It is crucial to affirm ourselves with positive thinking and self-talk. Numbers 13:33 reads, "There we saw the giants (the descendants of Anak came from the giants), and we were like grasshoppers in our sight, and so we were in their sight." A grasshopper mentality can kill your potential faster than what anybody says or thinks about you.

Your perception of yourself is often projected on the world around you. I had to realize that I was more than my mistake or issues. My identity is wrapped up in Christ in God, not in man's perception of me. The word of God says we all have sinned and come short of his glory, but must we continue in Sin? That's the big question of the century. I refuse to continue in Sin and frustrate the grace of God. Romans 6:1-3 Says being dead to Sin makes me alive to God. "What shall we say then? Shall we continue in Sin that grace may abound? 2 Certainly not! How shall we who died to sin live any longer in it? 3 Or do you not know that as many of us as were baptized into Christ Jesus were baptized into His death?" We cannot use our liberty as an excuse for sin any longer. The anointing is never a license to act in a way that is unbecoming of a child of God. Our titles are merely titles; it is our character that must stand alone on the day of judgment.

Being born again is the qualification for inheriting eternal life, but it does not stop there. We must practice living and walking in the Spirit. The anointing empowers us to live a life of power, breaking and destroying the yoke of bondage in our lives. It allows us to do great works and administer healing and deliverance to those in need and ourselves. The Holy Spirit empowers us to live holy, but only if we submit ourselves to His leadership and guidance. Everything is based on choice. We can choose to allow God to control our every existence, or we can choose Satan to control us. This area of my life is under the blood and at the feet of Jesus. I will no longer be controlled, manipulated, or deceived by the devil, others, or myself. The word of God in Galatians 5 says; "Stand fast therefore in the liberty by which Christ has made us free, and do not be entangled again with a yoke of bondage. Its Over! Whom the Son set free is free indeed. Today I made the choice to be free and so can you.

Let us Pray:

Father, In the name of Jesus, we come before you, giving you thanks and praise for our well-being. Thank you Lord for delivering us from the plans and plots of the enemy. Thank you for not allowing the enemy to keep us in bondage. Thank you for making a way of escape for us. Forgive us of all our sins and cleanse us from all of our iniquities. We repent and confess to you as Lord of our lives. I pray for the person reading this prayer; they feel like they can't survive or will make it out of what they are trapped in, but God, you are a mighty deliverer. Please give them the strength to walk out of what many have died and were held hostage to.

Lift them on every side and give them peace. As they cast all their cares on you, Father, show them you are a loving and forgiving God. Break the Spirit of idol-ship off their lives. Break the Spirit of perverseness, filthiness, adultery, idolatry, fornication, sex addiction, and whoredom off their lives. Heal them in areas that are hidden from the naked eye. We surrender our will to your will and our thoughts and actions to your thoughts and actions. Cleanse us from the filthiness of our flesh and spirit. Create a clean heart and renew the right a right spirit in us.

We break the cycle of repeated bad behaviors, habits, and the spirit of lasciviousness off our lives by the power of the Holy Ghost! No more death and toxic cycles. Blot out our sins and transgressions. Wash us from all uncleanliness. Father, forgive us once again as we forgive others and ourselves, for your grace is sufficient, and your strength is perfect in our times of weakness. We decree and declare that we shall live and not die to declare the will of God in our lives. We thank you for our new beginning. We thank you for our healing. We embrace our new season and is excited for what is to come. Our deliverance starts now! Thank you for being a faithful Father; in Jesus' name, we pray, Amen.

About The Author

Louiciana Joseph

Louiciana Joseph was born in Freeport, Grand Bahamas. She is the daughter of Haitian Bahamian descents. She is the third of five siblings and was known to be the shy and reserved of the group. Despite her introverted nature, she aspired of becoming a cosmetologist, police officer, or private investigator. While in high school she pursued a career in hair styling and earned an associate degree in private investigation from City College in 2006. Later, she obtained a bachelor's degree in biblical studies from Harvest Christian University. Louiciana is a teacher by profession. She is board certified in her VPK Credential, Staff Credential, Directors Credential, and Child Development Associate Credential.

In addition to that she is the proud mother of two beautiful daughters, Dominique and Alexandria, and a granddaughter by the named of Harmony. Ms. Joseph is a believer and a devoted Christian. She is an ordained minister of the gospel of Jesus Christ and is affectionately known as "Pastor CeeCee" within her circle. She is an active member of Kingdom Worshippers Church Int'l, under the leadership of Apostle Dr. Ricardo Strachan. She holds the position in her ministry as the assistant director of the single ministry. Pastor CeeCee is a prayer warrior and a woman of faith. She empowers and encourages others by ministering the word of God as occasion demands. Her goal is to serve God and fulfill her assignment in the Kingdom.

The Author's Information
Louiciana Joseph
Email: Louiciana34@yahoo.com

Thank you for purchasing this book.

Publisher's Information
MPC Creative Publishing & Designs LLC
Email: mpccreativepublishing@gmail.com
Ph: 954-479-2563

I Will No Longer Be Your Secret!

Made in the USA
Columbia, SC
22 July 2023